Sanjiv Sarin retired in 2019 as CEO and MD of Tata Coffee Ltd after forty-two years in corporate life, which took him to senior leadership roles through four continents. Earlier he spent seventeen years with Cadbury where his last assignment was as Country Director, Philippines.

He is currently an Independent Director on the board of companies and a Trustee with various NGOs.

He is a certified Leadership Coach and is the Founder and CEO of Purpledot Consultants in the space of coaching.

As a student, he had a stellar academic record, earning the Bombay University Gold Medal for Masters in Economics, and later earned a distinction at the Masters in Management Program from the Asian Institute of Management, Manila, Philippines. He was awarded the Triple A (Alumni Achievement Award), the highest recognition given by the institute to its outstanding alumni.

He was awarded 'CEO of the Year—Food and Beverages' by the World Quality Congress, the 'Udyog Ratan Award' by the Institute of Economic Studies, and 'Exceptional Leaders of Excellence' award by the Women's Economic Forum.

Sanjiv became a teacher with the Art of Living Foundation in 2001.He has also been the Joint CEO of Corporate Programs, and a Trustee with the Philippines Chapter.

He lives in Bengaluru, India, with his wife Vandana.

Connect with Sanjiv at: linkedin.com/in/sanjiv-sarin-30a2083

Praise for *The Other Side of the Mountain*

The Other Side of the Mountain is a deeply moving journey into self-discovery, spirituality, and purpose. Through personal reflections and transformative experiences, Sarin invites readers to explore the beauty of resilience, love, and inner peace. This book is an inspiring testament to the power of introspection and spiritual growth, and it offers a guiding light for anyone on their own journey of self-awareness and enlightenment.

—Dr Marshall Goldsmith, Thinkers50, #1 Executive Coach and *New York Times* bestselling author of *The Earned Life, Triggers,* and *What Got You Here Won't Get You There*

In this moving and powerful book, Sanjiv Sarin demonstrates how spirituality and business can and do coexist. It is a wonderful illustration of how we do not need to compromise, and instead do good *and* do well.

—Dr Tal Ben-Shahar, Co-Founder Happiness Studies Academy (USA) and former lecturer at Harvard University

The Other Side of the Mountain by Sanjiv Sarin invites readers on a transformative journey that intertwines the rigours of corporate life with the profound depths of spiritual exploration. Through candid anecdotes and illuminating insights, he shares his experiences in the world of business and his pursuit of success while discovering a deeper calling—a quest for inner peace and purpose. Sanjiv inspires readers to redefine success on their own terms and seek harmony between professional endeavours and spiritual fulfilment. His journey challenges conventional notions of success and reminds the readers that true fulfilment lies not just in what we achieve, but in who we become along the way.

—Sanjiv Mehta, Executive Chairman, L Catterton India,
Former Chairman/CEO and MD, Hindustan Unilever Limited

From a bright spark at Hyderabad Public School to a valued corporate leader in India's leading business group, the Tatas, Sanjiv Sarin has lived a life of achievement and excellence. Yet, he has remained rooted in the social milieu around him, shining light on the importance of spirituality and commitment in a competitive business environment. These highly evocative and impassioned notes from a life well and truly lived should be read by everyone who seeks work-life balance, negotiating the here-and-now and the thereafter. Read, learn, experience and cherish this book.

—Sanjaya Baru, Former Editor, *Financial Express* and
Business Standard. Former Media Advisor to
Prime Minister Manmohan Singh

The Other Side of the Mountain is a remarkable memoir about a life that climbed one side of the corporate mountain only to find, by looping around to the other side, a path to fulfilment and deeper purpose. Through candid insights, the author shares lessons from a career spanning continents, leadership challenges, and a life-altering moment during the November 2008 Mumbai terrorist attacks. His journey reveals how spirituality—when seen as self-connection and clarity—can be a powerful tool in business and life, helping us find balance, resilience, and true success.

This book is an inspiring guide for anyone navigating their path, from young professionals to seasoned leaders, showing how the summit of personal and professional fulfilment is best reached by climbing with intention, self-discovery, and humanity.

—Naveen A. Rao, MD; FACP, Senior Vice President, Health, Rockefeller Foundation, USA

Having seen Sanjiv up close and personal, I have seen first-hand both sides of him and the gradual transition to 'the other side'. I can, therefore, attest to this very personal memoir. The flow is engaging and full of anecdotes and experiential learning. The one phrase that immediately jumped out to me was, 'Spirituality is about connecting with oneself.' Rarely are books this personal. I encourage any person seeking fulfilment to read this.

—Ajay Nanavati, Former MD, 3M Israel,
MD 3M India, Chairman, Syndicate Bank

The memoir is a very engaging, unpretentious, and brutally honest account of the spiritual journey and how it shaped the life and attitude of a successful corporate honcho. I like the openness with which Sanjiv has shared the journey, punctuated with real instances, and how he has contextualised spirituality. His articulation is simple, clear and sharp, with brilliant nuggets of wisdom and insights. There were a number of déjà vu moments as I read through. I genuinely wished I had the benefit of these insights and perspectives earlier on in my own corporate journey.

—Bhaskar Sharma, Senior Advisor, Red Bull India & Business
Consultant. Former CEO Red Bull India

Sanjiv has generously shared his journey with authenticity—and, in the process opened up spaces where the spiritual intersects life, thereby becoming part of life. A memoir that is both everyday and special, and has the quality of relatedness that is easy to connect with.

—Vinita Bali, formerly in leadership roles with Cadbury
Schweppes, The Coca-Cola Company and Britannia. Presently
Independent Director on Indian and international boards

A vital testimonial on how the other side of the mountain—of spirituality—can not only power us through the mountain of corporate leadership but also can help us enjoy and experience the panoramic beauty on both sides. Through rich anecdotes, disarming honesty and pearls of practical wisdom, Sanjiv takes us through a fascinating journey on the path less travelled to live fully the path we all traverse.

—Sanjay Pradhan, CEO, Open Government Partnership,
Former Vice President of Leadership, Learning,
The World Bank Institute, The World Bank

Sanjiv has been a friend, philosopher and guide to me over the last twenty-five years. I have, therefore, seen very closely not only his evolution and growth but, beyond that. I have personally experienced his ability to contribute to mine in a holistic way. His approach has been to ask searching questions in a gentle but firm manner and be there for you whilst you find answers that are yours.

Whilst laying out his transformative journey with great vulnerability in *The Other Side of the Mountain*, by asking the right questions, he manages to make the reader go within herself, to find answers and trigger the start of potential transformation. That is the power of this book and something

I have experienced first-hand and for which I express deep gratitude to Sanjiv.

—Abhik Mitra, Former CEO, TNT India. Founder and former CEO Spoton Logistics. Currently Operating Partner and Head Operations Samara Capital

The Other Side of the Mountain by Sanjiv Sarin is a unique book by a corporate leader...deeply personal, it's about a redefinition of success, how a great corporate career (and a successful climb up the ladder) and a spiritual 'career' can co-exist. Read it not to learn the 'x number of rules of success' but to learn and be inspired by the enmeshing of two paths—the mercantile and the spiritual.

—Rekha Menon, Independent Director, Legrand, Biocon, Invest India, XLRI, Advisor, Apollo Healthaxis, former Chairperson and Sr Managing Director, Accenture in India

The Other Side of the Mountain

A CEO's Journey Through Spirituality

SANJIV SARIN

SPEAKING TIGER

SPEAKING TIGER BOOKS
125A, Ground Floor, Shahpur Jat
New Delhi – 110049

First published by Speaking Tiger in 2025

ISBN: 978-93-6336-332-8
eISBN: 978-93-6336-504-9

10 9 8 7 6 5 4 3 2 1

Typeset in Perpetua by SÜRYA, New Delhi

Dedicated to

My parents who gave me the gift of life

My wife Vandana and our children who have walked along with me through this life

Gurudev Sri Sri Ravi Shankar for unfolding the beauty of life

Contents

Gratitude

How do I thank Gurudev Sri Sri Ravishankar, who took me through the journey of building self-awareness, self-belief and sensitivity without me being aware of the transformation happening?

My learnings came from observing him, reading, and listening to his talks, which led to a lot of introspection and application of the learnings in my life. The only way to embed learning is to apply it.

My coming onto the path was not serendipity because it is said that the Guru, like the sun, is always there. The link happens when you are ready. The clouds disappear, and the sun comes through bright and clear.

My way of expressing gratitude is to walk the path and share the impact it has had on me with others. It is with this gratitude that I write this memoir.

Foreword

In this lovely book, Sanjiv Sarin invites us to climb the mountain with him, and view the other side. It is a beautiful and a therapeutic view, because the green valley that he shows us can rejuvenate us and bring great calm and joy into our lives.

Every page in this book holds a human insight that is born from our deepest desires and anxieties. Sanjiv Sarin has lived a rich life, both on the pathways of business and spirituality, and he writes frankly about the many crossroads and dilemmas that he has faced. He dips deep into his experience to bring the reader a distillation of some of the lessons he has learnt, and then provokes us to think about the same lessons in the context of our own lives.

I have known Sanjiv Sarin for nearly a decade, during his long and distinguished career with the Tata group. Throughout that long period, I could see that he dealt with some of the most challenging situations with a thoughtful intellect and with the utmost determination—but, even more importantly, with a calm mind and a heart of gold. I had always wondered where these qualities came from.

Now, reading this book, I understand how Sanjiv's voyage with the Art of Living Foundation has had such a profound impact on him, and has helped him view the other side of the mountain so clearly and at a relatively young age. The point that he makes to us in this regard is simple and powerful. We need to pursue our professional goals, but we also need to set ourselves human improvement goals, that will help us become far better and happier people.

Written in a lucid style, this book flows very easily. Sanjiv's simple narration, peppered with real-life stories from his career, makes it a very engaging read. Each theme—whether it be managing anger or giving it your best—resonated deeply with me, because these areas are so relevant to my own life. What has however impressed me most is the 'emotional content' of this book. What Sanjiv says in these pages awakens the mind, but also provides the mind broad pointers for crafting the way forward. The questions that he then poses to the reader at the end of each chapter help to provoke us into discovering our own solutions.

Some of the stories he has narrated here surprised me. Until I read this book, I did not know, for instance, that Sanjiv was in the Taj Hotel in Mumbai on 26/11, the day of the terrorist attack. His ability to stay completely tranquil and peaceful through that terrible episode, until he was rescued, fascinates me. It however reaffirms my belief that deep within Sanjiv's tough, professional exterior there is an island of calm. He has demonstrated this several times during the years that I have known him.

These are memoirs, and yet they are more than memoirs alone. Because in these essays and reflections you will find a refreshingly candid guidebook for life. Thank you, Sanjiv, for writing from your heart.

HARISH BHAT
Former Brand Custodian, Tata Sons
Avid marketer and bestselling author

1

It Happened at the Taj Mahal Hotel

Mumbai, 26/11

In early 2008, I returned to India from the Philippines, where I was the Country Director at Cadbury Adams, and joined Tata Coffee Ltd as Executive Director, Projects. I was based in Bengaluru and travelled weekly to Mumbai. Sometimes, it was a day trip; often, it was for a few days. At this time, the Taj Mahal Hotel in Mumbai became a second home. The hotel knew my love for the sea-facing rooms and always provided me with one. To wake up in the morning and see the gentle waves roll in or the fierce ones pounding the city in the monsoon time was breathtaking. Little did I realise at the time that this love for the sea-facing side would prove to be a lifesaver.

I was staying at the hotel on the fateful night of 26 November 2008, when terrorists attacked multiple locations in Mumbai, including the hotel. The story of how I survived the attack is a combination of miracles, the ability to keep a calm mind, deep surrender, and the prayers of my loved ones.

It was around 9.30-9.45 p.m. on the Wednesday night. I was watching the India–England one-day match on TV, lying comfortably in bed in my bathrobe on the third floor of the Taj Heritage wing, after a bath and dinner. I heard loud cracking sounds outside the room and wondered what was happening. Was there an event in the ballroom downstairs, and were guests having a gala time? It did not seem likely, so I opened the door and heard the loud barking of dogs and a whole lot of what sounded then like crackers. Had I been dressed, I may have gone to the central aisle to see what it was all about, but being in the bathrobe possibly saved me. I shut the door and called the reception, but there was no answer. I made a local call from my mobile to the Taj and was told to stay indoors and keep the lights off. There was a problem.

So, I lay in bed watching the match to the end, with constant gunfire outside. I was not able to fathom what was happening. Just as the match finished, I got a call that there was a terrorist attack. I switched on the news for two minutes before the signals were scrambled. I called home and spoke with my wife Vandana, telling her to switch on the news. And then the long night began.

With the lights and the TV turned off, the room was now in darkness. The silence was broken by loud and consistent gunfire outside the room. I heard explosions, glass shattering, and footsteps running outside.

Phone calls from family and friends kept me awake and informed. I made calls to the hotel telephone operator, and, God bless her, she answered. She kept advising me to keep the door locked and not to open it till she said so.

Smoke was billowing in, and my eyes were starting to burn. My children advised me to put a wet towel at the bottom of the front door and another around my face. They suggested I go back and sit on the ground behind the bed in case there was a crossfire and I got caught in that. I did that, and waited patiently.

The thought kept crossing my mind—I hope I am rescued before the terrorists break in, or the smoke suffocates me.

I put on a pair of trousers and a shirt just in case I needed to evacuate the room quickly. I packed my bags, the laptop, and put a visiting card in the bag and wrote my name on the labels so the baggage would be identifiable when rescued.

After that, I sat on the bed and went into meditation. I switched on my iPod, and the first discourse of Sri Sri Ravishankar that played was 'Intention, attention, manifestation'. It was exactly the space I was in.

My mind stayed calm, alive, and sharp, saving me. Meditation is the power of silence, the power to explore within and connect with the infinite life source surrounding us.

Early the next morning, Vandana called me from Bengaluru to say the fire brigade had come in to rescue the in-room guests. She was obviously watching it all on TV. I saw them from my window, going up and down in their rescue platforms bringing people out from the rooms. I then saw them approach my window and I gave them a thumbs-up sign to tell them I was well and signalled to them to rescue others first. They did and then came back, broke open the window, and pulled me out.

The memory of that moment when I stepped out of the third-floor window is permanently etched in my mind. I will always recall standing on the rescue platform of the fire brigade, watching the burning tower of the Taj as I was brought down.

The saga ended, but the memories stayed. The sound of a firecracker going off would unnerve me for a long time. A month after coming out of the Taj, I felt the need to return there, so I could immerse myself in the surroundings, confront any remaining fears, and heal from within. I had to focus my mind and face challenges; otherwise, they would have engulfed me. The process was cathartic.

My family and close friends helped me survive and recover by making me stay centred, accepting the situation, and taking positive action. I also felt the presence of grace guiding me. I am deeply grateful to everyone who supported me that night.

The meditative, tranquil mind saw me through.

Business travel was a necessity and my life went back to its previous routine. My single thought from that experience was to search for my purpose in life. Why did I survive?

My life's journey thus far had brought me to this point. Let me take a step back and describe it, and then reflect on how a subsequent journey was constructed.

2

Stepping Back

Life is a great and wonderful journey, and the time of youth is a free-flowing period of exploration, when the future is an open expanse of possibilities. The journey that connects the now to the future is filled with so many twists and turns, highs and lows; so many 'Aha' and 'Oho' moments!

The challenge and joy lie in navigating this path—exploring, finding yourself, transforming along the way, and ultimately achieving some kind of fulfilment. Many people are in a state of exploration at different times in their lives. Some start early and some come to it late.

I had forty-two years of a successful corporate life, which took me to different continents in senior leadership positions with Cadbury and Tata Global Beverages before I retired as MD and CEO of Tata Coffee Ltd. Along the way, I was given the Triple A (Alumni Achievement Award) recognition from the Asian Institute of Management, Manila, my alma mater. It is the highest recognition given to its outstanding alumni.

I entered the industry as a young, carefree Management Trainee and experienced tribulations and uncertainties early on. I was strong academically, and I wanted to explore how to do good for humanity, but I ended up meeting what seemed to be the hard-nosed realities of business. Over a period of time, I climbed the mountain and saw the other side.

What I experienced on the other side was a space of evolution—it enabled me to understand myself, what I was seeking, and what was important to me. When you reach that space consciously, it is a moment of freedom because you are attempting to script the path yourself and are not led by the environment. Today, I am a certified leadership coach helping business heads unravel issues they struggle with, just as I have managed to do in my career. It is a calling to be there for them in their journey.

Decades ago, in 1996, life led me on a spiritual journey midway through my career. This resulted in my evolution into a calmer, more focused person and gradually onto the path of humane leadership. I could also experience the changes it was creating in my relationships, my commitment at work, and the quality of delivery.

The path to inner stillness brought me there, and it was the same still mind that was invaluable as I emerged safe and sound from the Taj Hotel after the 26/11 terror attack.

The purpose of this memoir is to share some of my distilled learnings and how they changed my attitude and enabled me to embrace a fulfilling and successful corporate life. It is not a prescription but one person's journey, which was supported by many people and experiences. Long ago, there was a book, *What They Do*

Not Teach You in Harvard Business School, which contained skills and lessons learnt beyond academia. Similarly, this brief memoir is about what I learned and how it changed my attitude and approach at the workplace.

Change is possible; you just have to keep yourself open to what comes your way.

I have mentioned that I embarked on a spiritual journey; but what is spirituality? It is an oft-spoken term, yet it frequently remains shrouded in mysticism and seems out of reach.

To me, spirituality is about connecting with oneself—decluttering the mind, clearing away confusion, and being open to experiencing the joy in the little things around us: the flowers, the fresh air, the environment, and like children, being fully immersed in the moment. It's about appreciating the small treasures in life.

Spirituality enables us to empty our minds and sharpen our focus on what truly needs to be done. It emphasises the importance of being accountable and demanding performance while also appreciating the human behind that. It fosters awareness, allowing us to respond thoughtfully instead of merely reacting.

It is about knowing, accepting and believing in oneself.

Importantly, spirituality is not about renouncing life and retreating into solitude. It involves actively engaging in society while maintaining calm and equanimity. Life will always present highs and lows, but spirituality enhances our ability to recover more quickly from the lows and extend the highs.

First Steps on the Spiritual Path

My spiritual evolution began by me following my wife Vandana's explorations. Eventually it took me deeper, leading me to join the Art of Living Foundation, a deeply spiritual movement that promotes global peace, helps people to manage stress, and enables them to embark on their spiritual evolution. Possibly, I was also subconsciously in a state of readiness to embrace this.

In 1996, I had a narrow escape while playing with our kids in a swimming pool with a tall water slide. I climbed up and came down the slide—the last thing I remember. Next I was lying flat on the ground outside the pool and the kids were pumping water out of me.

The CT scans were clear, so I continued my whirlwind travelling on work. But my sleep patterns were disturbed, and my ability to focus was low. Once back home in Mumbai, I got an MRI, which showed some blood clotting in the brain as a result of an internal injury. The neurosurgeon called me a walking miracle as I had survived despite all my running around. I had to take eight weeks off from work for recovery.

The incident spurred Vandana to explore the transitory side of life and the possible loss of a loved one. She had lost her father at the tender age of eleven, and suddenly, life seemed ephemeral yet again. Vandana began attending several life-purpose programs and was recommended the Art of Living program by a dear friend. I decided to join her for this one, to understand her explorations. I do not know why I chose the Art of Living program and not any other. Little did I realise this marked the beginning of my own spiritual explorations.

Life was never the same after that.

Vandana decided to take the Art of Living Advanced Course at the Bengaluru ashram. Six months later, an Advanced Course was taking place in Rishikesh, and I decided to go there. She asked me why, and I had no answer.

I flew to Delhi from Mumbai and got on the bus taking devotees to Rishikesh. Right through the drive, people were singing bhajans, and I was cringing—what had I gotten myself into? We reached Rishikesh late evening and I recall asking my seatmate enroute if there would be food when we reached. She answered, 'Wait and watch.' I was focused on practicality, and here she was, telling me to drop it and be with the experience—to let things unfold.

One day at the program, Sri Sri Ravi Shankar, the Founder of the Art of Living, was leading a session and speaking about people going to therapy to address early life issues like relationships, expectations and their impact. 'We cannot change the past,' he said. 'Accept and move forward. Nobody wrongs you wilfully; understand the circumstances.'

My ears pricked up. It felt like he was talking to me because I had been tackling some issues of neglect in a relationship. I got into a question-and-answer session with him, and for the next few minutes, it was as if it was just him and me and nobody else. Then, suddenly, like a hammer on my head, there was clarity that the neglect had not been intentional. That moment was the start of a great healing within.

I vividly recall him asking me: 'Did you get what you came here for?'

Was he prescient?

I still recall his statement, 'The role of the Guru is to enable the journey from the head to the heart.' While I did not appreciate the true depth of this statement at the time, it started a journey that would change my life forever.

One evening during the program, it was raining, and the satsang was moved to the hall. The singing was evocative, and sitting there, my whole body filled with an electric charge and my eyes welled with tears. I could not fathom what was happening, and it rattled me.

In those days, Sri Sri would meet participants in small groups. There were four of us. As we entered the room, one of the four burst into tears. This caught me by surprise, and I wondered what had transpired. It so happened that Sri Sri asked him to become a teacher.

Out of curiosity, I asked Sri Sri, 'What about me?' He just looked at me and said, 'Do some more courses.' He could obviously sense at what stage of evolution a person was in.

I left the course a few hours early. Sitting in the boat crossing the Ganga, I felt a torrent of uncontrollable tears flowing, a deep emptying, and yet a fullness inside—I was empty of doubt but filled with an overwhelming feeling of love.

The journey on the spiritual path had begun.

The journey that began thus culminated in my becoming a teacher of the Art of Living five years later.

Many years later, I was with Sri Sri in Moscow. I recall asking him, 'You have taken hold of my finger—where are you taking me?'

His answer still rings in my ears: 'To the right place.'

My Sister's Influence

My sister, affectionately called Guddi by everyone, was my 'Living Buddha'. Guddi was a child with learning disabilities. I say 'was' because she passed on in 2021.

As a kid growing up, I did not understand what 'mentally challenged' meant. My sister was variously referred to as mongoloid because of her facial features and mentally retarded because of her very low IQ level. I recall being told that her mental age would not cross that of a six-year-old.

To me, six is the age of innocence, when one is still driven by the simplicity and transparency of the heart. It is also the age of intransigence when there is obstinacy and childlike demands for attention. Rationality is not part of the repertoire. The child responds with her emotions. That is the mental age she stayed in perpetuity.

The world began changing and referring to these children as 'challenged' and then as 'children with special needs'. To me they are 'children of a special god' and not of a 'lesser god', who have come into our lives to teach us deep lessons of love, patience, acceptance and service.

My childhood years with her were confusing. There was some anger because of the special and differential attention my parents gave her. Everything revolved around her, she could never be wrong and we needed to accept that. Yet there was a very strong protective feeling and an anger in me if any outsider mocked her. I recall we would drive to pick up my mother from the school where she was teaching. All the kids would run after the car screaming 'Daboo Seth has come' translating into 'the fat one has come'. You had to be there to feel my anger.

Gradually, growing up, I began to acknowledge that she is who she is and the special care she needed to look after herself and have society accept her was inevitable. It was important that I be comfortable with her, for only then would others accept her. I also began to appreciate the effort my parents were making to integrate her into society. In doing that they were also training us for future responsibilities.

She was full of love and openly displayed her emotions—give love, receive love. She had her unique language, which we could understand, but most others could not. My understanding came from being with her, living and experiencing her emotions, and deriving the situational reference behind what she was saying.

There were times she tested my patience with her intransigence, knowing she could easily get away. But being with her taught me empathy, and I learnt conscious listening and patience.

She was free-spirited, living life as it unfolded in the moment. Planning for the future was left to us. Music and passionate dancing defined her. She existed fully in the here and now. What happened in the past did not exist, at least not in her conscious communication, and I do not think she had a plan or thought about what tomorrow meant or would bring.

Yet there was a deep sense of the spiritual within her. I recall this incident from 1971, when Guddi was ten years old. The family was visiting Bengaluru and we went to the ashram of Sathya Sai Baba in Whitefield as he was in town. We joined the group of people waiting for his arrival. He walked onto the stage and lo and behold my sister went prostrate. None of us had told her about him and there she was flat on the ground. She never failed to amaze me.

My angst about her slowly shifted to accepting her, to being there for her, and deeply loving her.

Acceptance revealed the reality of her dependence and the purity of our love. It also opened my heart to those who need that little bit more understanding and support. It got me to devote time to the Sadhana School in Mumbai which is a well-known school for children with special needs. Ever since then such institutions have been intertwined with my corporate life.

I started committing time to Sadhana School by being there with the children. As part of my support, two friends and I developed a website for the school, which we named 'You give me wings'. This was at the early stages of the digital era and it highlighted the school's commitment to development needs of these children. The school added a section 'Friends of Sadhana'. It was a heartwarming moment for me to be there on the page with the likes of HH Dalai Lama.

Guddi would join us for dinner at the table. On the top of the cabinet in front of her was the statue of a reclining Buddha. She would continuously look at it and address it as 'Chotu', which is a friendly and loving way to address a young one.

She would talk to herself but with her eyes fixed

ahead. I discussed this with the principal of Sadhana School who mentioned that such children could well be communicating with an alternate world. Their mere presence teaches us many life lessons.

My lesson was she opened my heart to myself. She taught me immense patience and how to be there for those who need care.

These were possibly the first stirrings of a spiritual dimension in my life.

Stringing Invisible Strands

I did not think I was spiritually inclined until I began to reflect and see the patterns much later in life. Prayers were always present at home but never imposed on us. It was a daily morning ritual for my father. After bathing, he would chant and pray in his small temple in the bedroom.

Our home was a rational one. I do not recall too many rituals or spiritual discussions. It was more important to learn the English words in *Reader's Digest*'s 'It pays to increase your word power' and read the newspaper.

In my early school years, I recall we would go to a temple on some Tuesday evenings. It was a given that the family would all go together. I had no calling. Now, looking back, I think all these must have left some impression on my young mind.

I went to college to St Xavier's, Mumbai, and stayed in the hostel. Amidst all of life's distractions, three or four of us would sometimes walk across in the evening to a nearby gurdwara, sit there for about thirty minutes, and soak in the peace. It just felt very nice.

Many years later, I was on a flight from Hyderabad to Cochin via Tirupati. We landed in Tirupati, and the aircraft, strange as it may sound, had a flat tyre—this has never happened again in all my years of flying. The spare had to be flown in from Chennai, which gave us the whole day free. Indian Airlines organised a coach and thus I had my first darshan at the Tirupati temple.

One day, during a working visit to Kanyakumari, I took a ferry across to the Vivekananda Math, a small island about ten minutes away. I went as a curious tourist. At the Math there was a quiet room with a dim green light. It was so silent, peaceful and inviting that I just sat inside, not wanting to get up and leave. There was an overwhelming feeling of peace and well-being. This was well before I heard the word 'meditation'.

Work took me to multiple places. Once, I visited a famous and revered temple. As I sat down to attend the prayer, a few temple workers gathered and offered to show me the 'inner corridors of the sanctorum'. They took me through the dark, isolated corridors of the temple, and every now and then, they would stop, do some prayer, and make me pull out money. There was nowhere I could go because it was all dark, and there were these very hefty people surrounding me. It was scary. I exited with my wallet cleaned out, scared but alive and relieved.

That experience kept me away from large temples. It was a rude shock that places of worship could be so mercenary. Yet, it did not stop me from seeking out the smaller ones where I would go and just sit and soak in the peace.

Many years later, and now married, my wife Vandana was keen to go to Vaishno Devi. Another couple joined us, and off we went. Did I have a calling from the goddess? Not that I can remember. It was a good trek up the mountain. It was freezing cold, and it snowed on the way down. I am consciously calling it a trek because it was the companionship and mountain climb that were the highlights for me, not the 'overt' faith. Yet, a feeling of peace came back with me.

Then work took me to Egypt. While there, Vandana and I walked up Mt Sinai, where Moses received the commandments. We started the walk at 1 a.m., reached the peak at sunrise, and then walked down again—a total of eight hours. And it happened to be Easter. I did not realise the significance of the day until we had come down the mountain.

How did we choose Easter? And what made me do this 'all night' walk? Yet again, it was Vandana who led the exploration.

We were once at the Harmandir Saheb, Golden Temple, Amritsar, sitting in the sanctum until late evening, when they carried the Granth out for the night, and then at 4 a.m., they carried the Granth back into the sanctum.

We made a spur-of-the-moment visit to Gurudwara

Nanka Sahib in Pakistan, the birthplace of Guru Nanak, while we were in Lahore.

And we sat through a service at the Notre Dame in Paris.

All these at the insistence of Vandana.

In 2005, we were living in London when Pope John Paul passed away. I could not resist getting on the Underground train and attending his commemorative service at St Paul's Cathedral.

Many years later, during a conference in Kolkata, the entire team was on a night cruise on the Hooghly River. There was intense partying, as often happens after a hard day's work. The boat meandered along the Hooghly, and suddenly, in the distance, I saw what looked like a magnificent structure. It was the Dakshineshwar Kali temple, one of the Adi Shakti Peeths. So strong was the pull that early the next morning, I hired a cab and drove down to spend time there.

I recall another incident when I was flying from Delhi to Kathmandu. As we approached the foothills of the Himalayas, I felt a strong connection that I belonged there. It was momentary. The flight landed, and the thought also passed with it. I did not pay much attention to it, but the thought kept returning periodically. Many years later, in a past life regression session, I saw myself as a pandit sitting among the fields at the foothills of the Himalayas, reading some scriptures.

I have rarely been gifted books, but three serendipitously came my way, adding to the spiritual thread building up unknowingly: *The Third Eye* by Lobsang Rampa, gifted in the early 1970s by my brother; *The Autobiography of a Yogi* by Paramahansa Yogananda sometime in 1980s; *The Celestine Prophecy* by James Redfield in late 1990s, which was given to me by the HR Director at Cadbury. I again ask myself the question: Why these and not any bestselling management books? These books intrigued me, but I left it at that.

When I string all these experiences together, it is evident that while I always considered myself a logical, left-brained, rational person shunning ritualistic spaces, something kept pulling me to spaces that emanated peace. I must say that Vandana played a significant role in these explorations. Many a time, I went only because of her. I was mostly following her. Once inside, I would drift into silence. I suppose there is truth in the saying: 'There are no coincidences.'

Things happen for a reason, and looking back, a picture emerged for me. It made me wonder what drove me to all this. When did I shift from being a tourist in the spiritual realm to a seeker? Was I on a spiritual path all along but never acknowledged it? When did it unfold?

Temples, gurdwaras, churches…to me, these are merely places of silence and peace. What is important for me is the oneness of everyone, being with and in touch with the self, and being of service to others.

Interestingly, I have been praying silently at night before bedtime since I was a child. The two lines of prayer, with a little addition, are still a part of my litany today.

It feels like spirituality had been inadvertently following me. Eventually, it caught up with me, and we moved together for a while. Now, there are moments when I feel like I am pursuing it because it always seems to be a few elusive steps ahead of me.

Explore: What dots and transition moments can you connect in your life? How have they shaped your journey?

3

Some Early Explorations in Spirituality

My mother tells me of this incident that happened long ago when I was about five or six years of age. We were in Delhi and it was peak summer. She and I were outdoors, walking in the oppressive heat, buffeted by hot winds and under the blazing sun. She says I requested her to use an umbrella while walking outside otherwise she would be taken up straight to God. We always laughed it off as words of an innocent child, which they could well have been. But now when I think back, were those words evidence of some early stirrings of the spiritual path?

I have been driven by a need to know more about myself from an early age. When I joined college, I did personality and aptitude tests at the Student Counselling Centre. I repeated the tests at the end of the undergraduate years to see how I had evolved and if my interests had changed. I continue this exploration of changes, if any, in my values, interests and what drives me.

Many years ago, I did a note to myself, calling it 'My experiments with the heart'. I quote from there:

'When you follow the heart, there is an intrinsic internal capability that takes over. Because of your belief, the world helps you along. You help yourself along too. Believe in yourself, every time. I did take that risk on myself and life blossomed.'

The risks I have taken are varied—I left a blue-chip corporate to pursue an MBA mid-career in Manila. I went there with Vandana, our one-year-old son and a serious deficit in funding the program. My mother-in-law was in a state of shock, and people said I had taken a bold decision. The dictionary explains 'bold' as 'showing a willingness to risks' and does not say 'a great choice'. With those words flooding my mind, I ran into a dear friend's father at an airport and told him what I was doing. He shook my hand and said, 'It is the best thing you have done.' I wanted to hug him for that positive endorsement and the power of his words have stayed entrenched in me.

Interestingly, subsequently a leading multinational wanted to recruit me because of my self-belief and the risks I had taken for my self-development. You have to back yourself—otherwise why will anyone else?

Understanding the 'why' of my actions has been important to me. I make time to reflect during my evening walk, when I think on words that I have read or just let the thoughts freely crisscross my mind. Or I sit quietly by myself and contemplate.

Music began as something fun. I learnt a few guitar chords and songs in the long break we had after finishing school. This was great for camaraderie, but gradually music became an important source of 'me time'. I would pick up the guitar and just play around randomly, and that would bring a reflective calm. Many years later, I went onstage, a couple of times, to sing for an NGO to help it raise money for thalaessemic and cancer-stricken children who were below the poverty line. It had evolved into music for a purpose. Tata Coffee ran a school for children with learning disabilities in Coorg. Many a time Vandana and I would go there in the evenings and sing along with children. The enthusiasm and joy in these sessions was contagious.

The constant questioning through introspection has created many moments of clarity. Some of this is reflected in the pages ahead.

> Explore: What is your 'me time'? How did the reflections that popped up during this quiet time guide you forward?

4

Align the Head, Heart and Hand

During my undergraduate years in the early 1970s, I was involved in a multitude of activities—General Secretary of the Student's Union Council, playing for the college tennis team, debating—a group of close friends and I were just experiencing life. Academics felt like a cakewalk and I would even coach a few of my batchmates. I was honing my identity and resumé to catapult me into my future. It was very satisfying to perform so well at St Xavier's College, Mumbai, having come from a relatively smaller town like Hyderabad.

I was pursuing an undergraduate degree majoring in Mathematics with a subsidiary in Economics. Life was fulfilling, and I felt an aura of invincibility. I experienced amazing growth, and the world was out there to be conquered.

There is a history to how the Bachelor's degree in Mathematics and Economics came about. Just after school, my father presented me with the Nobel Prize-winner Paul Samuelson's book *Economics: An Introductory Analysis*. I enjoyed reading it, and something attracted me to the subject. Joining St Xavier's was meant to be a path to take the entrance examination for the Indian Institute of Technology, a far cry from Economics. In those days, IIT was one of the automatic choices for the competent. Even as I thought I was on the path to the IITs, I began to explore the choice, by speaking with IIT students about their experiences. A friend had exited within six months, another was unhappy. They spoke of stress. Maybe the chosen sample was small, but they were my 'influencers'. I changed my mind and reimagined my journey in Economics. A major in Mathematics provided me that opportunity without losing a study year. It was a trade-off between doing Mathematics, or losing a year and shifting my study stream from science to humanities.

Mathematics required consistent effort and a deep understanding of principles. I had not prepared myself for that, and my active 'non-academic' life began to overtake me.

To prepare for the final graduation examination, I began to rely on tutorial books with model answers that solved the previous year's examination papers. These were shortcuts, and I was very good at solving them. Had the structure of the paper stayed as per past trends, life would have been glorious. However, on the examination day, I found a new mix of topics and questions. This caught me off guard, and my performance dipped.

I felt anger, pain and frustration. Had I focused excessively on extracurricular activities? Was it a case of tunnel vision, studying for the examinations rather than truly understanding the subjects?

I could see my future closing like in the movies—drawbridges being raised, locking me inside the fort, out of reach from the opportunities outside.

I felt rejected because I was finding it difficult to get subjects of my choice for my Masters. Here I was, a high flier from school, an all-around performer in college, but now struggling.

In hindsight, my approach to taking the shortcut caused the problem. However, hindsight could not solve the situation; it could only illuminate the future.

Sometimes, life gives you a second chance, and you must grab it. I managed to get admission into the Masters program in Economics, which was my dream and someone somewhere was listening.

I realised that taking shortcuts means short-changing yourself. Commitment and consistent hard work are important. Hence, when life gave me a second chance with admission into MA (Economics), the university library became my home, and I began devouring journal after journal.

As I explored Economics more deeply, I had multiple 'aha' moments. I was now appreciating and enjoying the subject. My understanding improved significantly, which positively impacted my in-class discussions. I even did a course in speed reading to arm myself with tools to absorb more and faster. My performance zoomed.

The result was I became President of the Economics Students Society and graduated with the Bombay University Gold Medal in Economics at the Masters level.

On reflection, I wonder, is hard work a sufficient condition? What drives the willingness to work hard, especially over the long haul? When does hard work not feel like hard work? The answer came many years later as I embarked on the spiritual path: The more you commit and immerse, the deeper your understanding becomes, making the journey more enjoyable, which in turn fuels your desire to delve even deeper. It creates a self-sustaining upward cycle.

Once you enjoy the path, it is no longer hard work. You love what you do, and you do what you love. The heart, mind and hand move in sync.

The heart embodies passion and the intensity of desire. Passion ignites focus and effort, transforming work into an enjoyable pursuit. The mind brings about intellectual commitment, and the hand performs the intensity of effort.

If the heart and mind are aligned, not the effort—success will not come your way.

If mind and effort are aligned, not the heart—you may get results, but there is stress.

If the heart and effort are aligned, not the mind—you do not know which way to go.

Looking back, I recognise that my heart, mind, and effort were not working in unison at the undergraduate level. When I was doing my Masters, the three were working deeply in conjunction with each other. Making sure they are aligned needs conscious effort. Aligning them is your responsibility, and only you have the capability to make it happen.

Look at sports people. Leading tennis players practise seven to eight hours a day. Would they be able to sustain such extreme effort if they did not love the sport? Observe marathon runners who practise endlessly for 25-30 km runs. How would they manage it without a love for what they are doing?

So often, you will hear your coach, teacher, or supervisor say: 'Put your heart into it.' It is for a reason.

When I was a teacher with the Art of Living there were times when I would get up at 4 a.m., carry printed fliers announcing courses, and reach newspaper distribution locations along Nepean Sea Road in Mumbai to ensure their insertion in the dailies. Then, I would return home, get ready, and go to work. The work was demanding, as I was heading Sales for a large multinational company.

There was a need to identify places to organise courses—people's homes, temples, public halls, etc.—and everything else that goes along with running a successful course. Straight from work, I would head out to run the courses. On some routes I would stop at a specific roadside food vendor, grab a bite, and head out to the location. It is admirable that Vandana encouraged me right through all this, though it meant spending less time at home.

I recall conducting a course in Byculla prison, Mumbai. It would start at 6.30 a.m., which meant leaving home at 5.30 a.m., running the course, rushing back home immediately after, showering, and getting to work.

Normally, this would stress anyone, but did I feel the pressure of the stretch? On the contrary, it was energising to be inside the prison with over eighty prisoners and see their transformation. It was gratifying and simply amazing. It used to fill me with deep gratitude that I had the opportunity to do this.

I did this because I wanted to, not because I had to. The latter blocks the flow of purpose. When you do it because you want to, you experience joy, ownership, commitment and high energy. Like I said, it is all about aligning the heart, head and effort.

I understand that this is easier said than done. Sometimes, you make choices due to various compulsions—external pressures, financial needs, circumstances, or simply a calling. Being aware of the reasons behind your choices makes it easier to handle them, and this awareness allows you to take supportive actions.

Explore: Reflect on the times when you felt things were not going your way. Where was the disconnect—heart, mind or effort? What would you do differently?

5

Dealing with Early Career Uncertainties

Industry was not my first choice of career. I had this immense desire to do something for society, be relevant, work in rural India, and create an impact through the social sector or in the Indian Administrative Services. I romanticised the District Magistrate role, and wanted to work in rural India, bringing about grassroots change. Maybe it was my limited exploration, but my vision of the IAS stopped at the DM's role.

Another part of me was driven by academia—a

strong urge to do a PhD—initially in Economics and then Business Management. I had grown up in an environment infused with academia. My father was a business consultant and professor of Business Strategy and Marketing for practising managers. We lived in a small community where our neighbours were doing similar work. The energy was infectious. The urge to be in academics stayed with me for a long time.

I explored, spoke with people, did a lot of self-analysis, only to realise these career options may not be a good fit. The romance of the IAS was till the District Magistrate level and in my view, academics would mean being outside the country if I wanted a successful career. As a fallback, I entered the corporate world.

During my postgraduate studies in Economics, I even rejected a leading MBA program. And here I was now, looking at the corporate world.

Over a period of time, I began to realise the importance of an MBA in the corporate world. Without a business degree, I would be at a disadvantage. So, I applied for an accelerated MBA program at the Asian Institute of Management, Philippines, and I also applied for a PhD in the US. During those times, there were foreign exchange restrictions and challenges in obtaining education loans. The MBA offer came in April, and I accepted it and flew off to Manila. In July, I got the PhD offer from the Kellogg School in the US, with a personal letter from the management guru, Philip Kotler. Sitting in Manila, I did not have the wherewithal to go through the process of clearances in India, so I continued at the Asian Institute of Management. There was deep regret for a long time for not taking up the PhD at Kellogg.

So, my entry into the corporate world was 'choice three'.

My initial working years were tumultuous. It was a 'perfect storm' with three forces striking simultaneously—industry was 'choice three', I was not an MBA, and my heart was in a PhD. And I dare say it did impact my performance. It did not end there. Even within the corporate world, my desire was to be in Marketing, the 'thinkers' space, but I entered the FMCG space ten years down in my career and into Sales. All these happened at different times but reflect a classic divergence between the heart, head and action.

That turmoil created significant uncertainty and stress. I cannot pinpoint how it manifested, but on reflection, I think it made me tentative and, at times, frustrated.

This was the conundrum: a person with a gold medal in Economics from Bombay University and a distinction from the Asian Institute of Management, not following where the heart wanted to go, hesitant and uncertain in the corporate world, and entering the FMCG world ten years behind his peers, most of whom had begun their careers in that division. It required a realignment in the mind to accept this, find my core strengths, and open myself into the growth mindset.

Very early in my career, my superior called me an 'enigma', and, at the time, it was probably close to the truth. (The dictionary meaning for enigma is 'something hard to understand or explain' and 'a mysterious person'.) I possibly treated the corporate world as an extension of the free-flowing college life, unlike an MBA graduate who had been through the grind and was hard-nosed about business. Possibly, I came across as a bright but casual person in comparison.

Intellectually I was applying myself. There was sharp understanding, analysis, strategic thinking, and innovative approaches, but on the inside, there was plenty of emotional turmoil.

This is when the Art of Living entered my life. I have still not figured out why. Was it waiting for things to boil over? They do say things appear when you are ready. This was 1996, and I was about to enter into a new phase of growth.

Explore: What movie emerges as you reflect on your life thus far? Did you feel some doors closing and unexpected doors opening?

6

The Path to Equanimity

Those were the days when I would pride myself on waking up at 4 a.m., driving for an hour to the airport, catching the early morning flight out, and being back late at night the same day after a whole day in the market or with the regional teams. I would keep a small notepad by my bedside in case a thought or reminder popped up during my sleep at night. And then, there were month-end calls to discuss targets. Life was stressful.

I think I was on a short fuse.

This was my life when I was introduced to the Art of Living, thanks to Vandana. My first experience of Sudarshan Kriya* was electrifying. The body was buzzing, and then the tranquillity descended. I fell in love with the calming after-effects of the Kriya, and I have done it every day since then, i.e. since October 1996 (well, almost every day).

My world was becoming calmer. Conversations began to change; feelings began to emerge. A softness was coming in.

Somewhere down the road, my kids began to tell me that I was becoming more 'human'. And kids are generally a strong bellwether.

Two conversations come to mind. One with the CEO of Cadbury. I had just returned from the Art of Living Ashram, and he asked, 'What have you done? You look ten years younger.' To me, it was a reflection of the energy and enthusiasm I was experiencing. My attitude was filled with positivity.

---

*Sudarshan Kriya is the rhythmic breathing technique taught by the Art of Living.

The other conversation was with the HR Director at Cadbury who came up to me one day and teased, 'You may be at peace, but at least ruffle up your hair so you look a little agitated.'

What was I feeling through this period? I was confused about what was happening within. There were times when music would bring tears to my eyes; I would look deeply at the resplendent colours of the evening sky and get immersed in the beauty; I was getting less agitated. But the word 'spiritual' was scaring me because, in those days, it was something outside corporate speak and considered 'airy fairy'. I kept this turmoil within, unsure how the corporate world would react.

I could feel a heightened sense of awareness and accountability. And I do not believe it was a coincidence that the deeper I got into the spiritual dimension, the greater was my upward career trajectory. In fact, my Art of Living teacher once suggested to me that maybe I was outgrowing the corporate world.

Was I?

Sustained meditation brings calmness and peace,

which in turn opens up time for unbridled reflection. It also sensitises and opens up the heart. A still mind is creative and reflective. It opens itself to seeing opportunity, beauty and humanness.

Explore: When was the last time you smelled the flowers, felt the air brush your face as you were driving or stopped to watch a sunset? Did you experience the calming rejuvenation?

7

Does Anger Manage You or Do You Manage Anger?

Anger is a natural emotion but for some it erupts far more severely and frequently than it does for others. When you are angry the body releases stress hormones like cortisol and adrenalin. These hormones constrict the blood vessels and force the blood to flow more forcefully, resulting in increased blood pressure. It takes time to come back to the normal state.

Anger creates irrationality and is often followed

by regret. It breaks communication and relationships. Needless to say, it also has a strong impact on the person who is at the receiving end.

I have been known, in the past, to be short on the fuse. It could be anger at a cab driver for charging the wrong fare. I recall my mother asking me to not get upset so easily. There was this very embarrassing moment where I had gone as a guest to a restaurant with my friend. It was a Sunday and the wait staff was obviously very busy servicing multiple customers. We kept calling them and they just did not come. I got up in a huff, knocked down my chair and grabbed the waiter by his arm. He was surprised, my friend was embarrassed, and I cringed later at my volatile display.

At work I would be stoic and suppress my anger so as not to disrupt the harmonious environment. But I was only building my stress levels and presenting a false persona. Pulling back from anger to normalcy is an equally long process. It is very difficult to hide the stress because it does show up in some other way—in your demeanour, or in your frosty approach. It makes for uneasy engagements and stilted conversations.

Very often, you get angry because of the unreasonable expectations that you have set on your team members. Have you understood the other person's capability? Do they have adequate resources and time? Sri Sri puts it very succinctly, 'Anger is the price you pay for other people's mistakes.' When you look at it through this lens, it makes you wonder if you should get angry.

You get angry because you have built an expectation. I recall I used to go to the Art of Living ashram in the evenings during some work trips. I would wait to meet Sri Sri and many times the meeting did not happen. This would lead to disappointment and frustration. One such evening, sitting at the airport, I switched on one of his lectures, and I heard him say something along the lines, 'You get familiar with a person and then expect special access,' and I realised the truth in that. Not meeting an expectation had created anger, but was it justified?

The familiarity and 'right to access' can, at times, make you take the other person for granted. In a decentralised, geographically dispersed work environment, it can get exaggerated. I recall my superior once telling me that one of the things he has to be careful about is the need to look over his shoulders and ensure that no one is taking shortcuts or doing something wrong under the assumption that they can explain away their actions later because they know the 'boss'.

Anger is certainly not conducive to building healthy relationships or creating a harmonious work environment.

If something is making you angry, you need to pause and observe what is getting you angry. Is there a pattern in the things that stoke the anger? Step back and look at the situations that create anger and distance yourself from the trigger so that they lose their control over you. No wonder, as children, you were told to count to ten before getting into a fight! Perhaps the person's behaviour that was the trigger was a one-off. Does that person need guidance, instead of anger?

The meditative mind allows you to become an observer and also reduce the expression of anger, if not completely eliminate it.

This is not to say you should become placid. There are times when you have to make your dissatisfaction known. 'Express anger but do not get caught in its emotion.' Conscious expression comes from awareness and does not let emotions cloud your judgement of the situation.

> Explore: Observe that moment when anger got the better of you.
> How did you feel? Would you like that to change?
> What will you do differently?

8

Change Starts Within You

These two powerful statements are embedded in me:

'What got you here will not get you there.'

—Marshall Goldsmith
(world's leading leadership coach)

'Something has to change for something to change.'

—Unknown

Being self-aware is a great start. Are you driven by the desire to become a better version of yourself? Do you constantly observe and introspect? Do you seek feedback regularly?

Growth happens in two areas—in technical skills or in human skills.

Technical skills are easier to identify and develop. Identifying human skills can be challenging, as often we are unaware of how our behaviour impacts others.

How do you identify what you need to work upon? Your team's perception of you is your reality. It is up to you to accept or reject this reality.

The Johari Window model* is a good tool to understand yourself and team dynamics. It is possible that you know your capabilities but others do not. How do you make others aware of this? So understanding the reverse is also critical—what are other people's views

---

*The Johari Window Model is a technique for better understanding of the self within a group dynamic. It was developed in 1955 by psychologists Joseph Lutz and Harry Ingham. The model is used to improve communication between group members and to enhance the individual's perception of others. It is based on the idea that trust can be acquired by revealing information about oneself to others and learning from their feedback.

about you that you are not aware of and how do you know that to identify your development path.

You spend your time trying to communicate to others your capabilities, what you have achieved, and why they should listen to and value you. You get into the mode: 'You listen to me.' But have you grown by doing this? Have you become a better leader? Have you become a better person?

It is so important to actively seek feedback on where you need to change. What are the habits that are irksome to others? What are your team members' expectations of you? It becomes very important to explore this space.

You have to identify what needs to shift and then walk the journey to embed the change. It does not mean you become someone who you are not. It means you should listen and accept what aligns with your inner self. I came across a very powerful statement which reflects a similar thought: 'Be who you are because other positions have been taken.'

Often, our ego prevents us from seeking or accepting other people's viewpoints. Our defences increase. We build guardrails around ourselves. Think: Do you possess the courage to accept that change is needed? Only after that can you commit to work on it. In my experience, change requires inner strength and grounding. And a spiritual path certainly enables this.

There was a time when my decision-making involved a lot of discussions with people, and I was proud that I was inclusive. There was a lot of prevarication—this or that and fretting about implications. There was no way to accurately predict the future. Yet, other people were left in limbo, awaiting a decision. I recall the CEO calling me up and asking me why was I not making a decision.

Yet another CEO gave me sage advice: 'Take a decision. It is okay if you have to change it later but at least people are not in a limbo.'

Both their feedback made me aware of the issue and its implications on the team. I was very conscious of this and over a period of two years my decision-making was considered speedy and sharp. All it needed was to become aware, accept the feedback and then make the choice to work on it.

At the end of every half-year review session with my team members, my standard question was, 'What can I do differently to improve?' The answers yielded some useful inputs.

One important feedback I received was that my thinking was complex, and I tended to connect ideas in a way that others may not follow easily. I tended to assume that everyone understood my perspective, which would affect my communication and the team's understanding. I had to make a conscious effort to bring others along with me, explaining step by step how and why I reached a decision. This feedback prompted me to make a conscious effort to change this behaviour, which I may not have realised without the input. I strongly believe that inner transformation is crucial for external change.

The important part is to actively seek feedback and create an environment where people do not hesitate to provide it, and there is no fear of retribution. People start to believe in you when they feel they are being heard and see a conscious attempt to work on it.

> Explore: How often have you sought feedback? How did that mould your growth?

9

Your Assumptions May Be Constraining You

In my early years, I kept my spirituality to myself, fearing that people in the corporate world would not understand or accept it. This inner conflict made me uneasy. I would attend meetings organised by the Art of Living but not speak about it. Similarly, I participated in satsangs—sessions of music and knowledge sharing—without sharing my experiences with others. I was living a double life, which stemmed from my own assumptions.

My life changed when I confronted those assumptions and began wearing the journey on my sleeve. Speaking freely about it made life transparent and so much simpler. My actions and demeanour came into alignment. People began to understand me better and I reduced my stress levels.

Similarly, often you live within your assumptions, which limits your actions. Check your beliefs and assumptions to see if they are valid. I came across an interesting statement: 'We judge ourselves by our intent and others by their actions.'

It is difficult to embrace what is new if the mind is cluttered with beliefs and ideas that you are clinging on to. We often categorise people based on our past experiences, their behaviour, or their position in the hierarchy. However, everyone, including yourself, is constantly evolving. How aware are you of these changes, and how quickly can you let go of previous perceptions? Being able to do this is essential for effective leadership.

You may have a jug of fresh orange juice in front of you, but you cannot drink it because the glass you are holding is filled with something else. You need to either pour out the contents of the glass or get a fresh glass. To refresh your mind, you must do so consciously and continuously. It is important to question your assumptions and to examine whether there is evidence to support them; if there is none, it is time to move on.

Are you aware that you may be operating on assumptions, or do you have a way to recognise this? Are you open to being corrected, and is there someone who will take the initiative to point it out to you? This can only occur if you have fostered an environment of trusting relationships where others feel safe to provide feedback and are motivated to support you.

You also need to have the self-belief and courage to accept that feedback. These trusting relationships are the source of strength for you and your team.

Let me provide an extreme example of how preconceived notions can affect decision-making. Many children have special needs, which can be either mental or physical. Often, there is a tendency to overlook the integration of these children into the work environment, under the assumption that they are not capable. However, when we change our perspective, we can see their significant abilities. Typically, when one faculty in a person is diminished, another tends to become stronger.

There are organisations that hire individuals with physical disabilities for roles that require verbal communication, such as telephone-based assistance. Similarly, some organisations have successfully trained individuals with mental challenges in skills like making handmade paper and catering. Numerous examples exist of highly successful visually impaired or physically disabled individuals who have excelled in various fields. N.S. Hema set up APD (The Association for People with Disability); Ray Charles was a blind musician; Stephen Hawking, a prominent scientist, was diagnosed with ALS; Helen Keller was the first hearing and visually impaired person to earn a Bachelors degree; Srikanth Bolla was the first visually impaired person to study business at MIT.

Recognising you are working on assumptions or constraining beliefs and then addressing them brings a sense of release and opens up new opportunities.

Explore: Reflect and become aware of a limiting belief. Engage with people to identify it. See how it is constraining your path. What can you do to address it?

10

Rest Drives Action

In my career, I have spent long periods travelling the country to meet consumers, working the markets, meeting small groups and interfacing with them. It was all about knowing the people, knowing trends, and picking up ideas to explore.

This was great, but it came at a cost.

My travel schedule would be four days a week, or an early morning out and a late evening return. It was physically and mentally exhausting. I would return and find my inbox choked with e-mails. I would be playing catch-up and accepting that many decisions had to be made in my absence. The stress was high. Of course, I had to learn to prioritise and identify the critical areas where I had to intervene.

While the frenzy of the pace was exciting, I am certain it took its toll over time. I am sure the quality of decision-making, communication and time spent with stakeholders would have suffered. There was this time when we were in half-yearly financial closing. I was stretched physically and mentally trying to get the company's sales numbers locked in. Costs got overlooked and were over the budget. I received a call from the CEO about this and I responded in a frustrated tone, something like, 'Nothing can be done now. I will look into it next quarter.' There was a frozen silence at the other end and it took me a while to unfreeze it. Ideally, there should have been a more transparent communication early on between us, so we could have aligned the leadership goals.

Along came the Art of Living, Sudarshan Kriya and meditation. They were a balm and enabled me to remain calm despite all the external chaos. They made me more productive because my mind was de-stressed and, therefore more focused and sharp.

People often asked me how I managed a senior corporate job while running courses for the Art of Living. My standard response used to be that a mind at peace adds many hours to a capable mind.

Sri Sri says it very beautifully: 'Believe you have time; don't let time manage you. You feel the pressure of time when you feel you cannot do something.'

My career saw a substantial upturn as a result. I recall a comment by my CEO: 'You have made a significant impact on the organisation.' It was not a small comment, I felt, coming from the head honcho.

Short bursts of stress and periods of high energy are helpful but cannot be sustained over the long haul. Why are poets and thinkers at their creative best when they are in a peaceful environment like by rivers, amidst greenery, or up in the mountains? A still mind is an energised mind.

Being focused only on the outcome can create stress. I recall month-end meetings to review performance.

They were more about numbers and applying pressure to achieve goals. I am sure those meetings were not exciting for the team until I realised that I can only impact what I control and I could only attempt to influence what I do not control.

You need to focus on expanding your circle of control—what actions you can take and what support do you need in order to do that. This shift transforms the meeting from a diatribe into a dialogue. For a while, letting go of the outcome can relieve significant pressure; it does not mean that results are not important. Concentrating on the steps you can take to achieve your goals is the true enabler, and also sets the mind at rest.

I hold Sri Sri's statement—'The deeper the rest, the more dynamic the action'—very close to my heart.

Explore: Step back and reflect on when you were most productive. Was it while you were in a state of calm or when under stress?

Compare the quality of output and team engagement when you are stressed versus when you are calm.

11

You Are Responsible for Your Reality

Accepting this truth is probably central to growth. Let me share different examples from my career:

In my early working days, I often felt wronged, and that had long-lasting repercussions. It made me tentative in my actions and made me constantly seek validation.

I was the only non-MBA in an organisation that prided itself on being a blue-chip recruiter of the best MBA graduates. Being selected gave me a sense of satisfaction, but it also left me and the organisation underprepared. They had expectations of a micro-level business understanding, and here I was, coming from the macro world of Economics, hoping the two would meet. Someone would say, look at the balance sheet, and I would run to the British Council Library to understand what that meant. It was important to work closely with my colleagues, sit with them to see what they were doing and share the workload to get a hands-on understanding. I could get the same information through discussions with the managers and that gave me an understanding, but it did not give me a hands-on experience of the process and it did not give me deep interaction with the staff. Hence it did not build their confidence in me. That is hindsight.

How was I responsible? Mentally, I had entered the industry as a last resort without fully understanding the differences in the way business graduates work from economists and without being aware of expectations. Coming into working life unprepared, I excuse myself, but it did have its impact.

Twelve years later, I joined Cadbury as Head of Sales for the Food Division. My first FMCG role. I seem to have specialised in breaking norms. My heart was in being a Marketing person, and here I was heading Sales. Yet, it was my choice, and I had to be responsible for it.

My desire to get into Marketing was becoming self-destructive. It was stressful; I felt locked in and frustrated at times, and I erroneously felt the company was not valuing me. However, the choice was mine. How could I hold the company responsible? I could have resigned, but a new organisation would take me for my sales experience. On further introspection, I decided to work to my strengths, which was as an analytical sales head, and it was best to be where I had built equity. As my mind shed its cobwebs, the wings started to emerge through the chrysalis. My attitude at work changed, with far higher engagement and positivity. Positivity is an upward spiral, while negativity goes the opposite way.

It showed up in the sprightliness in my discussions. I started to appreciate the organisation's efforts for me by giving me varied roles. And the organisation, too, started to see me in a very different light—highly engaged, competent, and delivering results. In hindsight, the varied roles made me a holistic business manager.

All this while, I knew I was delivering intellectually, but there was an emotional turmoil inside. I do believe I was limiting my opportunities because of this turmoil.

As I walked the spiritual path, I could feel the changes within me, and they were reflected in a subsequent statement by the CEO: 'You have made a significant impact on the organisation.'

The spiritual path had brought me there: Becoming calmer, taking responsibility for myself, and shifting my attitude.

The organisation was the same, but my worldview was creating a new environment. Since I was responsible for my blocks, only I could unlock them.

Explore: Where are you getting stuck? What role are you playing in perpetuating that?

12

Give It Your Best

I recall Sri Sri saying: 'If your heart is 100 per cent full, the mind is 100 per cent empty, and hands are 100 per cent busy, can there be any room for confusion?'

A 100 per cent empty mind is ready to absorb new thoughts, make new connections to information and is not stressed.

A 100 per cent full heart is a heart overflowing with love for humanity, it is sensitive to people. You value people for who they are and not because of the role they are playing in your life. This brings authenticity. There are no hidden agendas. There is trust.

Can you imagine Virat Kohli, Roger Federer, Sachin Tendulkar, Usain Bolt, Sergei Bubka and other champions like them saying they will not give 100 per cent on the field? They talk about being in the 'zone'—the state when you are completely focused. That can only happen when the mind is totally free from other distractions.

It is only when you give 100 per cent that you do not allow room for regrets. As the Bhagavad Gita says, you can only control your actions, not the result. Yes, your commitment to focused action brings you closer to the end result.

In 2018, torrential rains flooded Coorg, causing landslides and causing people to lose their homes. This was when I was CEO of Tata Coffee Ltd. One of the company's estates was also impacted. I visited the location and saw firsthand the impact of the floods on the people and the estate and the speed with which support had come. Workers had been evacuated and relocated very efficiently, and they were provided with food and shelter.

We conducted interviews with the affected workers and they overwhelmingly reported being unable to sleep due to recurring sounds and visions from 'that night'. I met Sri Sri, who suggested we do some interventions. A few Art of Living teachers in Coorg did some trauma relief programs for them.

We returned to the employees and learnt that 40 per cent reported better sleep. What about the balance 60 per cent? It was not acceptable. We went back and did some more work through the Art of Living, leading to 95 per cent workers sleeping well.

To me, giving it my all meant being there 100 per cent. We could have settled for just relocating people to safety. We could have settled for a 40 per cent improvement in sleep. But when we reached 95 per cent improvement in sleep, I knew we had given our best. That is when there were no second thoughts—no regrets, no wondering what more could have been done.

Look at children. They give themselves completely

to everything. The smallest of games is played with full engagement. They even cry with full intensity. They do not know what half-hearted means.

Explore: When was the last time you told yourself: 'If only I had put in more thought/ more effort...' Consciously convert that regret into a learning.

13

The Power of Self-belief

What is intuition, and where does it reside?

There was a time when I was very focused on analysis. It provided me with valuable insights and influenced my discussions and decision-making. Many of my decisions were guided by the Kepner Tregoe model*,

*The Kepner Tregoe decision analysis involves preparing a decision statement, defining objectives, ranking objectives, listing alternatives, scoring each alternative, choosing the top two or three alternatives, considering potential problems or negative effects of each, and analysing the weighted score versus the adversity rating for each and choosing the high-scoring one.

which I learned at the Asian Institute of Management. This model used weighted scores of 'Must Haves' and 'Wants'. However, many choices did not 'feel right'. The data would only slightly differ between two or three options. In these cases, the decision had to be based on a 'gut feeling'. So while analysis helped narrow down the options, it was only a guide. Ultimately, an inner voice and experience played a significant role in the decision-making process.

Many years later, Sri Sri shared that logical decisions are made through known information. However, known information is a limited subset of the cosmos of information and, therefore, limited in perspective. How do you tap into that large cosmos of information and guideposts? When do you stand firm despite known data going the other way?

This is not to deride data and analysis. They are critical and show the options clearly. Intuition is an amalgamation of analysis, bits of information collated somewhere along the way, years of understanding and internal churn, where patterns get embedded, dots join, and insights emerge. It is probably housed in wisdom. A calm, uncluttered mind is necessary for this to surface. It's like the difference between the tranquil clear waters of a lake versus a lake churned with gusts of wind. Nothing will be visible inside the latter.

Both intuition and conviction blossom in self-belief. Conviction leads to single-minded messaging, focused execution, and the ability to handle differing opinions.

Tata Coffee was a producer of excellent mass coffees. The internal systems were entrenched for that scale. Some of my travels into international markets showed green shoots of gourmet coffees emerging, small farms producing unique beans, cafes providing these to consumers at premiums, and the Internet giving consumers access to high-quality options. It only needed an open mind to connect the dots.

There was a strong belief that India's terrain and climatic conditions could not produce such beans. But the need was not for tons of coffee. It was to identify pockets where small and unique lots could be nurtured. It just 'felt' that this was a new direction to take.

Conviction means you do not give up, even if you are the last man standing. Single-mindedness, understanding capabilities, and right resourcing led to Starbucks, USA, accepting an 'Indian Micro Lot' of coffee for its 'Reserve' range. 'Reserve' is an exclusive range of coffees—small lots of the best coffees sourced globally from small farms. This unleashed a sea of energy within the organisation.

I have to admit there were moments of trepidation. Am I doing the right thing in pushing the system in a certain direction? Is there a golden pot waiting at the end?

I was going against the tide. Failure would have resulted in many 'I told you so' statements, my credibility brought into question, wasted effort and resources. Self-doubt did creep in. Had I really understood the opportunity? Did we have the capability to deliver?

Long ago, I came across a very powerful statement: 'You do not get a second chance to make a first impression.' This was that time for me. It was a high-stakes situation. Periods like this need a calm mind that can observe the external world and see patterns that create a leap into the future. Self-belief in these moments helps tackle the internal uncertainties and external chatter.

What differentiates successful entrepreneurs from the rest? A major reason is their single-minded belief in and pursuit of an opportunity. It is like a laser beam versus a searchlight. The former is sharp, focused, and therefore highly impactful.

> Explore: Reflect on your moments of success and observe the role intuition played in them. Are there occasions when you wish you had listened to your inner voice?

14

People Are Key

In corporate life, the journey of growth increasingly involves understanding that people must be valued over machines, finance and processes. Yes, machines, finance and processes are critical for success but they are finally managed by people. How you inspire people, facilitate their growth, and set examples are crucial for success.

One of the difficult aspects of leadership is asking an employee to leave the organisation due to non-performance or ethical issues. You tend to hesitate and avoid confrontation and direct communication. You are caught in a dilemma between the person and the organisation. The consequences of no action are bad for both the organisation and the person.

Let me share two instances from my working life at different stages of my spiritual journey that reflect the changes I was experiencing.

There was a non-performing sales leader, and there was pressure on me to take corrective action. After a long postponement and building huge internal stress, I called the person to come and meet me. The meeting was short, with no preamble; I just asked him to leave. I do not recall anything else from that meeting other than his tears. I did not see him again, and I still regret how I handled the situation. There should have been much more thought, preparation and counselling. I was not just terminating a work relationship but impacting a human life and his close networks. The way I acted resulted from being task-driven and not showing enough empathy. It did not make him or me feel good.

Much later, I again faced the underperformance of a very senior leader. The business was going adrift, and there was talk in the senior management that we needed to exit the manager. The easiest thing would have been to tell him things were not working out and terminate him. However, this time, I began digging in to understand the background. Interestingly, the person had been parachuted into the role to stop the financial bleeding in the business, which meant he had a strong performance record backing him.

He had put controls in place and had managed to steady the business. The organisation was now seeking growth; obviously, this person did not have the experience for this new phase. Nor had we trained him for it, so we were equally culpable. What message would we send out by terminating his employment? At one end, we had a person who had performed reasonably well but was now struggling, and at the other end, the team was struggling because the business was not growing, and the bottleneck was at the top. It was a turbulent time for me, trying to think of the right action. I was reading a book on leadership, in which HH the Dalai Lama is quoted saying that an action, however difficult on an individual, when it is good for the larger community, is okay. That confirmed we had to exit the person and set the right performance benchmark. Yet we had to be considerate of what he had delivered and the commitment he had displayed through the turbulence.

Leadership was pushing for termination, which I resisted. We relocated the manager to another location and in a role where his strength was relevant. He regained confidence.

The message was ultimately clear and impactful: we cannot tolerate non-performance, but we will treat each individual fairly.

In the first situation, I could not look the person in the eye again. In the second case, we remained collaborative colleagues. You have to do right by people. They are the core of a business.

Putting people first does not mean only being a support during times of crisis. It is about enabling them to grow, listening to them, and making them believe they matter.

During my first year at Tata Coffee, I met 250 managers in small groups of ten, cutting across hierarchy and functions. The purpose was to listen to them and seek thoughts for growth opportunities and the key irritants they faced in their work. It was clear that these meetings were a listening post and not a guarantee that everything would be acted upon. This clarity set the ground rules. The meetings provided a wealth of information for us to build an agenda.

The bigger win was the feedback from managers that they felt heard by the top decision-makers.

There was another time when I met with a few women employees and asked them how we can improve their work lives. This led to two policy changes: supporting a creche where children could be looked after during work hours, and allowing a young mother to travel with her baby and a caregiver for short business trips. The financial outlay was minimal, while the positive heft was big.

I mention these to underline the importance of listening and of genuinely caring for everyone in the organisation. Employees can see what is genuine and what is being done for effect. The former builds trust, while the latter destroys it.

I learned the importance of dealing with people in this manner very early in my working life, though it took me many years to embrace it deeply. In one of the assignments after my tumultuous introduction to corporate life, the head of the region opened their home for me to stay in. It made me feel like I belonged and trusted. It made me conscious of living up to performance expectations and not letting down the trust bestowed on me.

Subsequently, during my assessment, he made a comment that has stayed with me: 'Your knowledge is far greater in verbal discussions than in your written submissions.' In one sentence he had endorsed my ability and also pointed out the area that needed development. He had made an effort to understand me.

After all these decades, he is still the person who I revere, and it was his humaneness that left a deep impact.

Explore: What conflicts have you experienced in managing people and what were your learnings?

15

You Are a Good Human, Not a Superhuman

There was a time when I believed that as a leader, you need to have solutions for everything—that is what makes you a leader. That put a lot of pressure on me. Leadership is a high-pressure environment, and the added expectation I had created for myself only enhanced it.

Yet it is important to remember that you are as human as everyone else, with a set of capabilities and some areas of development. In an explosive world filled with information overflow and specialisations in diverse fields, there is just no way one person can be the fountainhead of all knowledge.

It is necessary to keep this in mind when you create teams and engage with people. Are you seeking clones of yourself, or do you want diversity? Often, people prefer working with teams with whom they are comfortable. However, is that important or should you be aspiring for teams with varied capabilities? You may not have all the answers, but together, you will have a better chance at success. Collaboration requires accepting the diverse capabilities and proclivities of people. We are all a mixed bag, and it is important to accept differences in people rather than attempt to make them clones of yourself. People will relate more to you if they believe you have innate faith in them.

Often, we believe that saying 'I do not know' is a sign of weakness. But is it? It requires a lot of strength and self-belief, and you need to be secure in yourself to say it. It is actually the exact reverse of weakness. It is at the heart of collaboration.

There is a famous saying, 'If you want to travel fast, travel alone; if you want to travel far, travel together.'

Any collaboration demands a 'low ego'. It is about shifting focus from 'me' to 'us'.

'Us' implies building a bond within the team while respecting individual competence. The relationship is the oil that smoothens the mechanism. You recruit for competence and then build a relationship. This is where a good human being shines.

As mentioned earlier, at the heart of building a relationship lies trust.

Trust is built by showing respect and care. It is important to interact with people without bias and to be genuine. People can tell if you have hidden agendas. It is crucial to be sensitive, listen attentively, and understand people's hopes and worries. Ultimately, it is important to deliver on commitments rather than just discussing them. Leadership is a constant responsibility, not limited to just the eight-hour work-day.

When competence and relationship come together, it is a winning combination.

In my own journey, there was a time when I

believed that only competence matters—being rational and focusing on work-linked conversations. When a manager told me that loyalty is important, I would dismiss his words. Over the years, experience taught me that competence and loyalty to the organisation are both important.

You cannot demand loyalty or insist that someone likes you. You have to inspire it through your behaviour. There is another famous line: 'Your actions speak so loud that I cannot hear the words you speak.'

People want to believe that their superiors are a mix of competence and emotions with vulnerabilities like everyone else. People want to feel engaged, heard, and cared for. They want a relationship with a human being, not a robot.

Sri Sri had once told me that spirituality is the journey from the head to the heart. I believe that leadership is that balance between the head and the heart.

Looking at the message ('what') rather than the messenger ('who') works for the best. The more open you are to the 'what', the more information comes your way. Very often, people get carried away by hierarchy (who said) or their personal biases (this person has an axe to grind). These create stress in the organisation and keep valuable information from reaching you.

Collaboration requires recognising the positive qualities in people and how they can contribute to achieving common goals for the greater good. When you focus on the positive aspects, your mindset shifts towards finding solutions instead of dwelling on obstacles. It also demands giving an unbiased ear to alternate viewpoints and having a willingness to take action only if everyone is heard and aligned. It is tough. It can slow you down, but the long-term power of this is huge. It is the difference between a car that is serviced and running with every part contributing to smooth movement, and a car stalling constantly because some parts are not functioning optimally. Just imagine driving a car with a flat tyre or with weak brakes.

As a manager you need to have an openness, an acceptance that you are one among everyone, and each one is there to contribute their best. It needs self-assurance, and a belief in yourself. You have to spend time individually with your team members to enable each one to be the best version of themselves.

For a long while, I was confused about ego and self-esteem (self-belief is at its centre). They sounded similar to me, yet you needed to shift from the former to the latter. I asked Sri Sri, and his answer stayed with me: 'Self-esteem is internally focused while ego is external.'

> Explore: How have outcomes differed when you managed from the heart versus from the head and heart? Which way do you tilt?

16

The Powers of 'YES' and 'NO'

These two words have strong reverberations but in opposite directions. They impact both the speaker and the recipient.

A 'No' to the recipient is a door closed. It puts guardrails around them and defines what they can and cannot do. It restricts creativity. It can be an energy downer, sapping them of any drive.

While I was teaching an Art of Living course, a participant related a very insightful story: John, a young boy, had parents who were always holding him back from doing things—no, don't do this, no, don't do that. Because of that, until age ten, he believed his name was 'No John'.

This story made me wonder about the impact 'no' has on a person's thinking and self-esteem.

There is a story about Thomas Alva Edison. His mother hid a letter from her son's school stating that the young Edison was 'addled' and would never amount to much. The mother did not accept the assessment and homeschooled him. His mother's support and belief in him made him what he was. His mother's 'Yes' mind enabled him to blossom.

Hearing 'no' means you will not stretch yourself to see how far you can go. Hearing 'yes' means you either do not perceive that limits exist, or you are free to stretch yourself to your furthest limits.

By saying 'no', you restrict your growth and possible exploration of solutions and opportunities. On the other hand, a 'Yes' mind says, 'I am there to support you. It may be tough, but we will work at it.' It puts you in control and tells the other person that they are supported. Your own mind opens to exploration.

Success needs a 'Yes' mind. It needs you to cut through cobwebs that may slow you down or cloud your vision and make you put on blinkers.

Is your mind a sponge filled with the waters of 'No' and, therefore, unable to soak in new ideas? You need to squeeze out the 'No's and then open yourself to receiving the power of soaking in the 'Yes'. The 'Yes' mindset is open, calm, uncluttered, and ready to take action. It fosters the courage to stand by your convictions. It is a 'can do' opportunity seeker.

In 1993, I moved to Egypt as Commercial Director of Cadbury Adams. At the time, the Art of Living was offering courses in Egypt, though infrequently, and they were conducted by travelling teachers. There was no specific place where the courses could be held regularly. I was looking for a location that could become the centre of activity and give it identity.

I took my chances and met a senior person at the Indian Embassy. I shared information about the Art of Living and the courses I was running in Cairo. Something struck a chord and this person allowed us to hold courses at the Maulana Azad Centre for Indian Culture (MACIC). The MACIC then opened its Yoga Centre for us, which became the Art of Living's home for the near future. None of this would have happened if I had been tentative. The mind would have created a chatter on why it was inappropriate, why the idea would be rejected, and why approaching anyone could be a waste of time. I was awarded the Cadbury Chairman's Global CSR award for all the work in Egypt for the Art of Living.

Consider the Paralympics, where athletes with physical disabilities perform at an extraordinary level. This accomplishment stems from self-belief and a strong 'Yes' mentality. Coaches embodying this mindset help transform abilities from disabilities.

'Yes' tells you things can happen against all odds. It drives innovation, change and growth. It forces you to think about how things can work, what could be the likely obstacles, who can help, what information gaps exist, etc. It is a great starting point. It attracts people and the environment to you because you are a supporter and a doer. It provokes you to give your best.

The power of the 'Yes' mind provides a smooth conduit between external opportunities and inward resources.

> Explore: Are you aware which mind space you operate from? Look around you and observe how people gravitate to the person with a 'Yes' mind.

17

Give of Yourself

Many people are searching for purpose in their lives and their work and seeking ways to integrate the two. Engaging with communities and supporting causes you believe in nurtures your well-being. This not only acts as a stress reliever but also enhances your engagement with the organisation when it supports these efforts. A corporation with a heart fosters a deep sense of fulfilment.

Contributing your time and effort is satisfying. You

can see the impact you are making. It could be supporting skill development for livelihood, educating kids who need the support, sustainability efforts, empowering the disenfranchised—the possibilities are endless.

Spending time with children at the Sadhana School was very satisfying and it was pushing me to do more. Setting up food camps in Manila through the Art of Living during the typhoons to support displaced people energised volunteers. I was observing the impact of 'giving'. Back in India, the Art of Living took me into lower-income communities to understand the lives of women who were dealing with a multitude of issues, from lack of finances to paucity of water in their neighbourhoods. These meetings shook me and the urge to make a difference increased.

It was a learning to see the people who volunteered in such areas work tirelessly and yet be energised at the end of the day. It was a validation of the statement that 'in giving we receive'.

During my time at Tata Coffee, the volunteer hours increased from around 300 to over 3,000. As employees recognised the organisation's strong support for volunteering, they began to propose projects that were meaningful to them. Many employees felt a desire to help others during times of natural disasters and expressed empathy for the communities affected by the disasters. When they were able to support relief efforts they found it uplifting and also demonstrated to them that the organisation truly cares.

It was also fortunate that the Tata Group has the ethos of supporting community-based initiatives.

As the leader of the organisation, you have to demonstrate that you believe in and will walk the path in meaningful endeavours. You have to demonstrate commitment. You do not have to be upfront. Let others take the lead, and you be the shepherd, keeping the flock together with gentle nudges from the back. People are happier and deliver better in a 'humane' organisation.

My journey has taught me that the more you focus on being there for others, the less the 'I' comes into the picture. It builds a stronger bond with the team and creates trusting relationships.

My forty-two years in corporate life has brought

many experiences. I have observed so much, learnt to grow, and have evolved as a human.

From a 'human being', I have learned how to be 'being human'. 'Being human' means acknowledging your existence on the planet. It means valuing yourself, having self-belief, and being empathetic. For me, it has meant believing in, valuing and being there for others.

In the process this has resulted in creating high-performing organisations.

I am quoting the then Chairman of the Tata Coffee Board and Tata Group Brand Custodian: 'Sanjiv was, and continues to be, perennially restless for the next frontier. He engages intensely with all stakeholders and pushes himself to raise the bar each year. Sanjiv also interfaces strongly with his community responsibilities. He has a strong spiritual bent that provides him with an inner calm despite the hectic and volatile pace that corporate leadership is inevitably faced with. He is a thorough professional and a genuine human being.'

Yet another comment was from a Director, Tata Sons Board: 'You have excelled in every assignment that has come your way.'

These words are a significant shift from being referred to as an 'enigma' early in my career.

In an interview I did with *Peak Life* magazine, I said:

'An organisation is a microcosm of the planet where human beings are at the core. Capital and technology can be bought. The human element determines what you make of them. Each person is here seeking happiness and striving to unlock their potential. It becomes so important, therefore, to enable people to blossom. And foster a space that nurtures collaboration so that jointly the organisation grows manifold and also becomes the place to be. Collaboration demands trust, transparency, building on each other's capabilities, each one delivering to commitments and beyond. Delivering ethically.

'The organisation has a social role to play in serving its communities. It cannot consume resources and not plough back. People are giving their active lifespan to the organisation and you need to enable them and their families to live happily. It demands opening your hearts beyond just profit and market share.'

My corporate journey, which was in tandem with a

spiritual pursuit through the Art of Living Foundation and its founder Sri Sri Ravishankar, showed me a powerful, sensitive and impactful path.

Epilogue

My spiritual journey along with the corporate life began in 1996 with my first Art of Living program while I was still working and continued until I retired in 2019.

This twenty-three-year overlap allowed both worlds to influence me deeply. Although this memoir is about the lessons I learned and applied along the way, much unfolded during the journey itself. What started as a way to relieve stress transformed into an exploration of the self and became a spiritual discovery. I still recall the title of Sri Sri's first lecture, 'Are You Tired?' and how it resonated, guiding me toward inner peace and a return to myself.

At the time, I was seeking mental clarity and was confronting my expectations. It was aggravating. The Art of Living softened me, while the corporate world demanded toughness. Integrating the two took time, but I eventually discovered that humaneness is a powerful way to achieve remarkable results while elevating the environment around you.

I struggled with committing to a spiritual master, questioning whether I needed one—or even the concept itself. Over time, I realised that throughout our lives, we have many teachers: parents, school and college instructors, mentors, and coaches. Every high-performing athlete has a coach guiding them toward success. So why not a coach for life, which often feels the most complex endeavour of all?

Once on the spiritual path, I learned that life is simple—we are the ones who complicate it. Having someone to help you declutter your life with no agenda other than your happiness has been invaluable.

As my priorities evolved, challenges emerged. I once

needed 'spirits' to feel high on life; now, life itself is my high. Some social situations felt awkward until I found my new equilibrium. Relationships with those close to me realigned, becoming deeper and more meaningful. Gradually, my self-questioning shifted from 'What do I need to succeed?' to 'What do I need to succeed and be true to myself?' This change was liberating, shaping my path, my choices and my decisions. It influenced the organisations I chose to be part of and the path I embraced after retirement.

When retirement approached, and I needed to choose where to focus, I asked myself the following questions:

— Will the chosen options bring me joy?
— Will they work with my natural talents?

From among the options I considered, four main directions emerged:

The first involved working with institutions supporting children with learning disabilities.

The second was educational support to children from the section that needs support. Capability is human, it needs an opportunity to shine.

The third was spending time coaching business and NGO leaders to become better, more impactful versions of themselves. Good leaders create expanding circles of positive impact

The fourth option was to continue teaching the Art of Living programs to help people destress and possibly take their initial steps onto the spiritual path.

Today, I find myself engaged in all the directions, each adding a new layer of meaning to my life. My NGO work has allowed me to witness the resilience and determination of children and young people with special needs. Their unbroken spirit and joy in the face of challenges inspire me deeply. It is equally heartening to observe the educators who dedicate their hearts and souls to helping these children become as independent as possible.

Through coaching business leaders, I have watched some individuals discover behaviours that are slowing them down and help them address these. I have also seen some find deeper purpose and together we have explored ways to integrate this into their lives. Their rewiring directly impacts the culture in their workspaces.

We have set up a family foundation which is at a very nascent stage.

Teaching Art of Living programs has been equally fulfilling, as each session reminds me of the profound simplicity of the spiritual path and its transformational impact on people.

What lies ahead for me now?

Perhaps more challenges and mountains to climb, though for now, they seem distant silhouettes.

Not long ago, I came across a powerful morning prayer that has become part of my daily routine:

'Waking up this morning, I smile. Twenty-four brand new hours are before me. I vow to live them deeply and to look at everything around me with an eye of compassion.'

In a self-assessment I did long ago, my 'signature strengths' that emerged were honesty, spirituality, hope, curiosity, humility, perspective, kindness and gratitude.

I look forward to integrate these with the prayer to see what connections come into my life. The spiritual path is not only for the 'Self' but also to create a positive environment within organisations and society—

the famous butterfly effect*.

The corporate world is increasingly embracing wellness and spiritual processes to cultivate positivity and in building an inclusive culture. Like individual bees that contribute to the collective hive, corporations must break silos to foster mutual support. This requires accepting diverse capabilities and setting aside ego, focusing on support rather than blame.

Spirituality is a powerful enabler of this shift.

I have seen relationships between employees and vendors strengthen as a natural outcome of shared sensitivity. Try searching online for 'how often do children smile', and you will find they smile about 400 times a day, compared to an average adult's 20. Embracing the spiritual path has the potential to reclaim some of those smiles for adults, too. Today's youth seek purpose beyond wealth and career; many take gap years to work with NGOs or support spiritual causes.

---

*The butterfly effect is a metaphor describing how even small actions can have far-reaching impacts, reflecting our world's deep interconnection.

Organisations need to recognise this and respond to it. A quick search for 'spirituality at work' reveals a wealth of material. Courses in positive psychology are spreading. Harvard's 'Positive Psychology' course and Yale's 'Psychology and the Good Life' have become their most popular offerings.

As I reflect on my journey, I see how the ripples of my choices continue to shape my life and of those I encounter. I am reminded that each day brings a new opportunity to deepen my commitment to compassion, purpose and growth. Through simple yet powerful practices like meditation, empathy and service, I hope to sustain my growth and embrace the future. And while I may not know what mountains lie ahead, I am ready to explore and embrace them with a heart full of gratitude and a mind full of curiosity.

Some Observations and Thoughts Along the Way

I have mentioned my 'me time' in one of the chapters. Thoughts come to me at this time, stirred by what I observe around me, life experiences or from something I read. I have long maintained a journal of these and am sharing a few of these little notes here.

Emerging from Under the Protective Tree

There was a big Gulmohar tree in our lawn. When in bloom, its flaming flowers brightened the place. Underneath the tree and along the fence there was a line of bushes that we were trying to grow in order to make a hedge. The hedge was lush except for the part under the Gulmohar.

One day, the tree fell. Within six months, the bushes languishing under the tree blossomed, and we had a flourishing hedge.

That got me thinking. How often do we stunt people's growth by being overprotective? People are waiting to find their place under the sun and realise their full potential. Our role is to enable this growth.

The Receptive Mind

We seek change, we seek the new, we want to reinvent ourselves. In the current work environment, reinventing ourselves, upskilling, and learning new skills is critical. Yet, the mind is preoccupied and cluttered with habits and thoughts of the way things have been—our tried-and-tested comfort zone. If the mind is already full, how will it open itself and find space for new thinking? Have you tried planting a seed without loosening the mud and creating space? The seed will not grow into a plant. Similarly, the mind needs to stay de-stressed and empty so that it is receptive to creative new thoughts.

The Shepherd

Ever wondered why a shepherd is generally at the rear of the herd and not in the front? Well, he is creating an environment where the more nimble and agile can run ahead so that others can follow them. Now and then, he runs to the front, taps the herd in a certain direction and then he moves back. This way, the shepherd manages to keep the herd in the desired direction and keep track of the entire lot.

The shepherd's role is to keep the herd together, keep everyone going in the same direction, bring back those who are wayward and motivate the flock to move together.

An effective team leader is exactly like this shepherd!

The Giving Tree

During a workshop some years ago, we were asked to hug a tree and observe it. It was a most elevating experience. Standing in the middle of a busy pavement and talking to a tree heightened and then quietened the ego.

Once the mind had settled, my eyes truly opened to the beauty of the tree.

Have you observed a tree closely and thought about the amazing life tenets it abides by and the life lessons it can teach? Animals scamper all over it. People treat it badly. Dogs urinate on it, parasitic plants live off it.

Yet, be it sunshine or rain, it does not flinch from providing shade and a resting space, cleaning the air we breathe, and selflessly giving of itself.

Imagine what the world would be like if we embraced this principle.

Row Your Boat Downstream

How often have we sung this as children: 'Row, row, row your boat, gently down the stream; merrily, merrily, merrily, merrily, life is but a dream...'

If you 'row your boat gently down the stream,' the journey will be smooth and the effort minimal because the stream is carrying you along. What if, instead, you try rowing against the flow? It will be tough.

Similarly, going along in the direction life is taking you becomes a pleasant experience. That does not mean you cannot or should not change direction, but you must be prepared for the rough and tumble of the journey.

If only someone had shared this with me as a child.

Reaching Out

Many years ago, XY and I were good friends, working closely together. But then we had a fallout. I got upset and stopped speaking with him. It was awkward because we had common friends, and yet even when we met in a group we would not address each other, or I would find reasons to avoid the gatherings. I was troubled, but I held on to the 'I had been wronged' syndrome.

Once I stepped back, I realised that I had not attempted to understand the circumstances and compulsions that created the issue. Was it a one-off, or was it repetitive behaviour?

I never thought about what XY would be thinking about me—that as a friend, I did not want to understand the pressures and compulsions he had been working under. I had conducted a one-sided trial and pronounced him guilty.

I was hurting, but my ego was holding me back from reaching out.

After many moons, I finally called XY. I felt a great sense of relief, and the response on the other end was similar.

Have you ever tried holding your breath for a long time? You can feel that inner pressure build up, and then there is such deep relief when you finally release the breath.

Let me share another instance. While teaching the Art of Living workshop in Cairo, I spoke about a similar circumstance and asked the group what prevents them from 'reaching out'. The next day, one participant told me that after the course that evening, she had made a call to a person she had given up on eight years ago. She was surprised and delighted when the person drove all the way to reconnect. Her phone call led to an eight-year hiatus being bridged.

We accumulate so much stress, and so many wonderful relationships are lost in the question: should I or the other person be the first to reach out? This happens at work and in personal life.

It is okay to be the one to reach out. You are the one benefiting. The past may not have been as you wanted but the future can be different. If nothing happens, that is also okay. You made the attempt and are at peace.

Getting Lost in Anger

Anger is an emotion that rises and subsides with a life of its own—or does it?

There have been times when my anger has erupted quickly, without my even realising it. In the aftermath I felt uneasy and embarrassed. In my coaching sessions, I often encounter leaders discussing their short tempers and the negative impact it has on their relationships. There are many reasons for this anger, such as failing to meet commitments, the pressure of deadlines, and not truly listening to what has been said. I have yet to meet anyone who feels satisfied with this behaviour.

There are two aspects to consider when it comes to anger: the feeling of anger and the expression of anger.

Generally speaking, people tend to express anger down the hierarchy rather than upward. For instance, you are more likely to express anger towards subordinates and peers rather than superiors. The mind is quite adept at distinguishing where anger can and cannot be expressed.

It is important to note that the phrase 'I lost control' may not tell the whole story.

But what are the consequences of expressing anger? The recipient may also feel shaken, stressed, pressured, rejected, or even guilty. None of these emotions foster a positive environment or support quality performance.

It is a lose-lose situation.

Along my journey, I realised something important: 'Respond, don't react.' This idea was probably first articulated by Stephen Covey, but my understanding deepened later through experience and conscious awareness. Reacting often means losing control, which can lead to actions we regret. Step back for some seconds and take a deep breath. Create distance from the situation. Be the observer. In that brief space of awareness, you are already in greater control.

There is a story about a well-known Indian business leader: A team member made a disastrous financial decision and was sure he would be sacked. However, the leader stepped back, acknowledged all the good things the person had done in the past, and saw his value. Grabbing that moment of awareness was the key.

You may still want to express your concerns in a forceful tone to make an impact. Go ahead and express those feelings, but do not get caught in the emotion of anger. That difference is significant. When this happens, the person at the receiving end is also in a better state of realisation.

That is a win-win.

The Authentic Water State

Do people know who they are interacting with when engaging with you? Are they aware of what you stand for? How different are you as a person at work compared to at home?

I remember intentionally distinguishing between 'the me at work' and 'the me at home'. I can even recall standing up in a meeting and proudly stating, 'I am a different person at work than I am at home.' While I don't remember the responses from others, this realisation stuck with me. At work, I was stoic, emotionally reserved, somewhat distant, and focused on tasks. In contrast, my home persona was relaxed, light-hearted and friendly.

Yes, there were many times when my work demeanour drifted into the home, and it was not very pleasant. I also had some people tell me to 'bring your personal self into work'.

What was I doing to myself by constantly switching between two personas? Who was the authentic 'me', and who was I presenting myself to? What masks was I wearing, and how often? I was definitely confusing myself and many others, and this was creating stress that I wasn't even aware of. In fact, I was actively encouraging it. It was like trying to walk on two tracks that would diverge further if left unattended.

Do you do this too? What impact is the shift having on the people around you? Which version of 'you' are they interacting with? Which one should they respond to? This interaction shapes their relationship with you.

Water exists in three different states: ice, water and steam. Each has distinct properties, and has different impacts—ice can cause frostbite, the liquid state can quench thirst, and steam can scald. Are people coming to you for a drink of water only to be scalded?

At Computer Point, I learned about WYSIWYG—'What You See Is What You Get.' It is important that people truly understand your intent and not navigate through ambiguity. It is crucial for your values to be clearly communicated. People need to know the guiding principles so they can navigate their relationship with you effectively. As a leader, you establish these value positions, so it is important to articulate them clearly.

Be authentic. It creates a culture that is easier to sustain.

Be your authentic water state and be a life enhancer.

Is It Okay to Forgive and Forget?

When a conflict arises, we are often encouraged to forgive and move on. Genuine forgiveness stems from the heart and leaves no lingering resentment. It is essential for your peace of mind, as well as for the other person. However, if negative feelings persist, the process doesn't fully resolve the underlying issue.

Forgiveness can mean, 'You are wrong, but I am letting go.' Isn't that still a one-way judgment followed by one-way justice? Sri Sri's words ring in my mind: 'No one willingly wants to harm. There is a victim inside crying for help. You just need to reach out, understand, and heal that space.'

Do reflect. There may have been times when you felt someone hurt you, and you only reacted.

You can explode and vent...but does that help? This can lead to a breakdown in a relationship.

For your peace of mind, you may forgive the other person, and on reflection find that it was not the person's normal behaviour. Has your forgiving spared the other person their guilt? Has he or she felt understood?

You can choose to reflect on the idea that a single action does not define a person and try to understand what triggered them. Were they dealing with a difficult situation in their personal life or were they having a challenging day? By recognising that there is a trigger, your anger can subside. This understanding might even put you in a position to reach out and help the person overcome their pain.

Look at some incidents from your recent past and see if the situations fit into any of the above alternatives.

Filling the Squares

I was reading the book *An Open Heart: Practising Compassion in Everyday Life* that contains extracts from the discourses of the Dalai Lama.

In one of the discourses, he says, '…self-confidence… is the basis of a bright future…Self-confidence is very important. How do we achieve it? First, we must bear in mind that we are equal to all human beings and that we have the same capabilities. If we remain pessimistic, thinking that we cannot succeed, then we are not able to evolve.'

Most of the time, the feeling of inadequacy and dissatisfaction comes up when we compare ourselves with others—be it work, money, or status. It is like holding a board with say, a hundred-plus squares. In each square you fill in your capabilities. In the end there may be one or two squares left empty. Those empty squares make you feel inadequate, and you end up making the full board about those few squares.

Stay within those limiting squares for a while and see how you feel. Do you feel depressed and inadequate?

Park those aside and focus on your unique and positive areas.

How does that make you feel? Liberated and joyous?

Be conscious of which thoughts you are focusing on. Remember, the thoughts you feed are the ones that will grow. So be mindful.

The Apprentice

Success does not come overnight when pivoting into the unknown. You could be moving from a corporate job to becoming an entrepreneur, or leaving a steady job to become a full-time musician. While there is excitement in the transition, you are leaving behind past successes and comforts. There will be periods of frustration and self-doubt because mastery is taking longer than anticipated or opportunities are not coming as fast as you thought they would. You end up dealing with uncertainty—did I make the right choice?

With any change, you need to embrace an 'apprentice' mindset. Learn the rules from ground zero, accept that it will take time yet willingly pursue learning, stay curious, keep up the enthusiasm and accept you are an 'apprentice'. It is like keeping the 'Learner' sign on the car as you learn to drive.

Faith with Eyes Wide Open

Recently, I had gone for a swim. After completing my laps for exercise, I relaxed in the pool while watching other swimmers and catching my breath. My attention was drawn to a young couple in the water with their two-year-old baby, who was wearing an inflatable suit. The father was gently guiding the child, helping him stroke the water and enjoy the experience. It was clear that the father was fully present with his son, and the child had complete trust in him—what I would describe as 'blind faith', because he had no other frame of reference.

There is a phase in life characterised by blind faith. Gradually, as we grow, our intellect takes over, prompting us to seek validation and experience to build trust.

Throughout life, we rely on various guides, including parents, teachers, mentors and friends. We admire them for their skills and the importance they hold in our lives. We choose these guides based on our needs, and they assist us during certain times, helping us to build trust in them.

We distinguish between people we trust and those we have faith in; many of us even possess 'implicit faith' in certain individuals.

Faith originates from our belief system. It is a permanent quality. Trust, on the other hand, arises from our relationships and is built over time, making it less permanent.

Faith can be seen as the highest level of trust. It involves trusting someone or something even when logic and evidence suggest otherwise.

For faith to flourish, one must be open and accepting. At the same time, the other person must exemplify trustworthiness, care, sensitivity, transparency, consistency, and an absence of hidden agendas.

This dynamic resembles the connection between a child and parent in the swimming pool, with the key difference being that we have evolved from 'blind faith' to 'faith with eyes wide open'.

Such a relationship sets us free.

Guiding Principles to Living with Intention and Compassion

- Meditate
- Be sensitive to others
- Serve society however you can
- Stay mindful of your actions
- Find your mojo because you control your life's path
- Connect your head, your heart and your hands

Acknowledgements

The idea for this memoir has germinated for over three years and has seen multiple versions. Friends and family have invested hours reading the various avatars and giving feedback about the content.

A few publishers I reached out to in the past told me to increase the word length, but to me, what I wanted to share was more important than how much I wrote. They did invest their time, and I am grateful for that.

I gave up on the idea of writing multiple times out of sheer frustration. At times, I would stop for weeks or even months. However, I continued to jot down my thoughts as they came to me.

Vandana encouraged me to keep writing and not give up. She shared insights from successful writers, emphasizing that many budding authors tend to quit midway due to obstacles or frustration. Her encouragement sustained my hope and helped me avoid taking the path to the exit, and ultimately, she succeeded in keeping me motivated. Her creative bent of mind constantly inspired me to think differently while writing the book.

Our children, Akshai, Aashrai, Pooja were always there to bounce off ideas and engage in taking the book to market. How can I forget Amar, our little grandson, who kept us cheerful through multiple video conversations.

One day, during my period of wanting to exit writing, I was on a call with Renooji (Renoo Nirula, a Spiritual Mentor), and she asked me how is the book coming along? She just said I must complete the book and that certainly refreshed my vigour.

Then came the other angel, Rugmani Prabhakar, a respected writer and poet deep into the spiritual path with the Art of Living Foundation. I was seeking advice from her about editing and other areas around publishing. She heard me out and gave me the relevant connections but called back the next morning, saying she would help with the editing because she understood me and the context. It was manna from heaven, and she has been an invaluable partner in shaping this.

Ravi Singh and Sudeshna Shome Ghosh, from Speaking Tiger the publisher of this book, played a key role in getting the book ready for the reader and bringing it to market. And another heartfelt thanks to Ravi for having faith in a first-time author.

I need to thank each of the people who have voluntarily read the manuscript and endorsed it. Some of them even made detailed notes in response. They are senior business leaders, and I am grateful they have taken the time. Also gratitude to all the business leaders I have worked with and who mentored me along the way.

I am grateful for the future support from those who will help share this memoir with readers and to the readers who will purchase and engage with the book. Thank you all in advance.

9 789363 360129

Printed at Repro India Ltd.